This book is a gift to you from Scottish Book Trust, a national charity changing lives through reading and writing, to celebrate Book Week Scotland (13–19 November 2023).

bookweekscotland.com

Adventure is a collection of true stories written by the people of Scotland. This book is one of 70,000 **free** copies – thank you for picking it up! If you enjoy it, help us share it with as many people as possible. Dip into it and share a few favourites with friends, display it, gift a copy to a partner, colleague or parent, or even leave it somewhere for a stranger to discover.
(We recommend a reading age of 15+.)

These stories are both funny and moving, paying tribute to the breadth of storytelling across multiple generations all over Scotland. If you enjoy this book, please consider making a donation so that everyone in Scotland has the opportunity to improve their life chances through books and the fundamental skills of reading and writing.

Visit **scottishbooktrust.com/donate** to find out more.

Happy reading!
#BookWeekScotland

A huge thank you to the following individuals who supported Scottish Book Trust as members of The Book Club

Gordon Dalyell and Pamela Leslie

Marian and Mark Deere

Martin Adam and William Zachs

Robert Hill

Scott Lothian

and those who wish to remain anonymous

Adventure

Book Week Scotland 2023

First published in 2023 by Scottish Book Trust,
Sandeman House, Trunk's Close, 55 High Street,
Edinburgh EH1 1SR

scottishbooktrust.com

A CIP catalogue record for this book is available
from the British Library

Typeset by Laura Jones

Printed and bound by CPI Group (UK) Ltd, Croydon CR0 4YY

Scottish Book Trust makes every effort to ensure that the paper
used in this book has been legally sourced from well-
managed and sustainable forests

Cover design by Craig Laurenson

This is a free book, designed to be read alone or in groups, enjoyed,
shared and passed on to friends. This book is gifted to you by
Scottish Book Trust for Book Week Scotland 2023

Digital editions of this book are available from
scottishbooktrust.com

Contents

Into the wild

New beginnings

*Stories by published authors.
Please be aware that this book is unsuitable for readers aged 14 or
younger as it contains strong language and mature content.

Ultraviolet
Elizabeth Craig

Glasgow, June 1967

3pm Saturday afternoon – The biggest adventure of my life is about to begin! I was seventeen last week, and my parents have finally consented to let me go to a disco in Glasgow. My excitement is off the scale. I feel like a proper teenager now, although I am lurching between elation at my newfound freedom, and terror as my adventure begins.

My hair is in giant rollers, and I am sporting a fetching quilted housecoat as I go rummaging in the wardrobe for a suitable outfit. I check my appearance every five minutes, because a giant acne spot is erupting right on the tip of my nose. I'm sure it's so big it can be seen from space. A carbuncle. Mount Etna. The end of the world as I know it.

4pm – Feeling more frantic by the minute, I phone my friends to ask for advice on said facial eruption. I get a recommendation to apply several layers of toothpaste, leave to dry, then to pile on the make-up.

5pm – My make-up bag spills a pile of brightly coloured lotions and potions across my dressing table, as I make my eyes black, my lips pale, and I have made sure that the carbuncle is buried under cement-like layers of toothpaste and foundation.

6pm – I backcomb my hair and apply half a can of lacquer, spluttering and choking on the fumes as I make a mental note to avoid naked flames.

6.30pm – With my hair suitably crispy, I don white knee-length boots, scoop up my coat and handbag, and attempt to leave the house avoiding my parents. I shout a cheerful goodbye from the door.

10 seconds after 6.30pm – I am summoned back by my father. 'What's that you're wearing?' he asks. 'Get a vest on under that. It's far too low in the neck.' In actual fact, it is a modest long-sleeved dress with a slightly scooped neckline.

6.35pm – I return to my room, carry out the prescribed changes to my dress code. A thick vest now peeks alluringly from my neckline. I pass muster and disappear into the night to meet my friends, resolving to stash the vest in my handbag at disco. I also resolve to remember to put it back on before returning home.

6.45pm – The adventure is about to start! Oh, my heart! I meet my friends at the bus stop and we do our customary greeting dance of jumping up and down while shrieking and laughing hysterically.

6.50pm – We clamber upstairs on the bus, all of us chattering at once.

7.15pm – We join the queue snaking up several flights of stairs to the disco, four storeys above. The giant spot on my nose is struggling to break loose from its bonds. We joke and laugh with the crowd whilst I secretly compare myself to the other girls, who all appear to be acne-free.

7.40pm – Finally, we get to the doorway of the disco. I am in need of oxygen after coming through the noxious blue haze of cigarette smoke on the way up. A large bouncer informs us the club is alcohol-free and asks if we have any contraband concealed about our persons. He fixes us with a long hard stare, and finally lets us in.

8pm – The vest is crammed into my handbag. Further lacquer is applied to my hair. More layers are piled onto the carbuncle. Extra glue is applied to my false eyelashes. A friend assists me by unsticking my top and bottom eyelids.

8.15pm – On the dancefloor! Motown music! Dancing round the handbags!

8.30pm – A handsome guy in a suit and tie asks me to dance. Hughie fae Easterhoose.

9pm – Hughie steers me to a booth and buys me a Coke. The ultraviolet lights above us turn my dress to an ethereal glowing robe. They also turn Hughie's fine set of upper dentures to a luminous array of tombstones when he smiles. Scenes from Dracula films flit through my mind.

9.20pm – My friend comes over from the dancefloor and hands me a mirror. Urgent whispers ensue. 'Take a look – you need to do something!' The ultraviolet light has illuminated the layers of toothpaste on the carbuncle, and my nose shines forth like a purple beacon.

Hughie and I smile at each other. We are bonded by our flaws. We look into each other's eyes. The light from his dentures and from my carbuncle combines, and shines around us. It is a wonderful ultraviolet aura of acceptance and lurve.

Author note: *My sister wrote a poem for my birthday, called 'Dancing in Glasgow'. It brought back a flood of memories, including this one, which, at the time, felt like the biggest adventure of my life.*

Smells Like Teen Spirit
Gillian Collins

There aren't many people dressed like me in my small Scottish town.

They don't get my funny big boots with the yellow stitching or why I might, on occasion, wish to dye my hair pink.

The taunts of 'goth' and 'weirdo' are hard at first. But soon, I begin to enjoy my moniker.

It means I'm unique.

Kurt Cobain says: 'They laugh at me because I'm different; I laugh at them because they're all the same.'

The bullies' lack of imagination and uniform of shiny flammable tracksuits only serve to fuel my teenage superiority complex.

For me, non-conformity is a salve to the banality of my small-town life.

My mum is perplexed that my bedroom walls are adorned with pictures of Kurt. Or as she would describe him: 'A very troubled young man.' I try to explain that he's a tortured genius but she can't understand why he has to be 'so depressing'.

I have a huge poster of him in my bedroom which I bought with my pocket money from Athena in the St Enoch Centre. Kurt's gorgeous eyes, lined with thick black kohl, stare back at me every night. It keeps falling down as it's so heavy and I am only allowed to use Blu Tack, because drawing pins will 'mark the wall'.

I want to buy the new Nirvana album but going up to the 'Big Town' is a big deal and it takes my best negotiation skills to convince my mum to let me go alone on the number 23 bus to Glasgow city centre.

The outfit for the trip is planned in great detail all week.

I've chosen the deliberately bobbly cardigan with holes poked through the cuffs for my thumbs. Scuffed-up leather boots with tartan laces (so quirky!) and a black velvet pinafore dress. Stripy black and red tights, reminiscent of the Wicked Witch of the West, finish off the look.

It is surprisingly time-consuming to look this dishevelled.

The weekend takes forever to come and when it finally does, I hop on the number 23 bus as though I'm a grunge version of Christopher Columbus off to discover the New World.

I'm a fearless explorer in an oversized cardigan.

I disembark on Hope Street and it is full of busy Saturday shoppers. An army of wee Glasgow wumin fighting against the wind and rain. They find shelter in What Every Woman Wants and start raiding the bins full of underwear and socks where you can get five for a fiver.

For me, the first stop is Tower Records under the Hielanman's Umbrella. An imposing yellow mecca attracting lots of people wearing those big funny boots with yellow stitching, just like me.

Most think it's just a record shop, but it's more than that. Carrying the yellow bag is the ultimate status symbol. It means you know your stuff. You are original. You are different. Like Kurt.

I position myself in the rock section to strategically demonstrate my exquisite and unusual taste in music. I pick up records that are popular, but not too popular.

Soundgarden is too mainstream. Pearl Jam is 'Dad Rock'.

I see one of those boys with long hair and green German jackets out of the corner of my eye as I elaborately paw *In Utero*. I'm too shy to speak to him, but I think he might have smiled at me. I hit a massive beamer.

The next stop is the legendary Virginia Galleries just off Argyle Street – a literal grunge nirvana.

The unassuming entrance hides the exotic world on the inside. A rainbow-coloured wall greets me, the staircase plastered with band posters for gigs at all the best Glasgow venues – The Barrowlands, King Tut's and The Rat Trap.

I climb the stairs and head for Mr Ben, where I rummage through the rails of vintage clothes. I settle on a '70s leather trench coat with a fur lapel. It has quite a pungent aroma, but a few skooshes of body spray sort that out.

As I make my way back downstairs I see him for the first time.

He's sticking up a flyer for a band.

Does he look a bit like Kurt Cobain?

Maybe.

He says 'hi' and tells me that it's his band and he's the lead singer.

He is six foot one, massive feet encased in sodden gutties. His jeans are baggy, his boxers on show.

He gestures towards the Tower Records bag and tells me his favourite band is The Smashing Pumpkins. I nod enthusiastically, pretending to have heard of them.

He plays The Rat Trap in a few weeks, he says.

He could put me on the guest list if I like?

There might be an A&R guy coming.

I don't know what an A&R guy is but I say 'that's cool' and arrange my face to look impressed.

He scribbles his number on the back of one of his flyers and pushes it into my hand.

I tell him I have to go.

It's almost five o'clock and my mum will go mental if I don't get home for tea. She's got a Marks and Spencer's layered pasta salad and chicken kievs in. We only get a Marks and Spencer's dinner on a Saturday so I can't miss it. I obviously don't tell him that.

He leans in and kisses my cheeks in that sophisticated French way which is usually supremely awkward for people from West Central Scotland. The tall singer carries it off and tells me to call during the week.

He smells of stale cigarettes and Lynx Africa. An intoxicating combination that would become the olfactory anthem of my teenage years.

Elated, I make my way back to suburbia on the number 23 bus. Back to Saturday night TV in my mum's living room, to *Casualty* and Paul Daniels.

I stick the flyer to my bedroom wall before I go to bed, next to Kurt Cobain's giant sad face.

My biggest adventure is just about to begin.

Author note: *So many great Glasgow shops and venues that served as the backdrop to some of the most defining moments of my youth are now gone. Places like Virginia Galleries, Tower Records and The Rat Trap hold so many memories. They offered a place for us to be ourselves, away from the restrictions of small-town life, where we could grow a counterculture that was uniquely ours. The story also pivots around the awkward self-conscious experience of my teenage years and the beautiful agony of first love.*

From Belfast with Love
Joanne Kerr

My friend Ann and I didn't take long to decide to
leave Belfast. It was early 1989 and we were in our
final year at Queen's University, not yet ready to stop
being students. We couldn't just google; there was no
all-singing, all-dancing website to explore. We had
brochures and leaflets with pictures and the edited
highlights of courses we could apply to. We didn't speak
to parents or seek advice from wise professors. To us,
it wasn't an adventure and there was no risk involved,
it was just the next phase of our young lives. We opted
for Edinburgh. It sounded like a good place to be, and it
looked very different from a run down and bombed-out
Belfast. Peace was still almost ten years away. We knew
very little about Scotland, just that it wasn't Northern
Ireland, and at the grand age of twenty-one, we decided
we were fed up with Belfast and all its troubles. We
were ready for something different. A new city, a new
university and a dream that only the young can carry
easily.

Our parents didn't intervene, they went along with
our plan and simply dropped us to the boat and waved
us off. I am sure they thought we would be home after
the year was up, ready to settle down. I don't remember
much about that boat journey, just that it was long and I
was wearing a very large rucksack which threatened to
topple me on more than one occasion.

We arrived in Edinburgh in August 1989, both of us
with a place at Edinburgh Napier (not yet a university),

and no idea of where we might stay. It's hard to believe now that our parents didn't worry about that, didn't ask questions or nag, and seemed to assume we knew what we were doing. We didn't. We registered at Merchiston and quickly got on a bus to visit our respective campuses. I was pretty delighted to find myself at leafy Spylaw, whereas Ann was less impressed with the faded glory and rambling Sighthill building. Suddenly conscious we didn't have a bed for the night, we started to consider our options. On the bus we met a friendly guy called Robert who casually advised that he had found a room in an old nursing home which was being turned into student accommodation. He took us there directly, and before it was dark we had both settled into student digs for the next year in a sprawling house near Bruntsfield. If my daughter told me that same story today I would be an anxious wreck.

Ann had won the toss for the best room – with the en suite – right beside the pay phone box and the front door. I had a smaller room on the second floor with a shared bathroom. There were eight of us sharing it and it wasn't always pleasant. It was a chaotic house, full of fun and drama. The alcoholic owner who lived there was a larger-than-life character who seemed to love and loathe us all equally. We were different from his previous house guests: we were loud, untidy, unreliable and I'm sure we were annoying as only students can be. However, he had his moments too, often with speakers blaring at 3am as he tried to play golf through an open window. Nowadays there would be regulations, health and safety to consider, fire doors and the like. We were just glad to have a lock on the door and a decent bed to sleep in. The best thing about that house was the large basement kitchen, which had been properly kitted out for the nursing home. There was a long refectory table and it was there that we met people from Nigeria, Malaysia, Greece and Germany. The world was at last becoming bigger, and there was a freedom in this city that Belfast had been unable to offer.

Edinburgh felt so very different to Belfast. At first it was the absences we noticed. There was no need to have your bag searched going into a shop, there were no soldiers with guns or armoured vehicles in the streets. We weren't wakened in the night by loud sirens and moved into the community centre. Instead, there was the Golf Tavern, which became an important meeting place – and where I was to meet my future husband. There were new friends from new places, the Meadows for lounging in the sun, a festival dedicated to laughter and life, and we also found time to study. It really was buzzing with hopeful energy. We had full grants and enough money in our pockets to live on, topped up with jobs at the Scotch Whisky Heritage Centre. Irish girls in kilts working as Scottish tour guides, whoever would have thought! That was a really special and unforgettable year, as we moved into adulthood.

I look back now at those girls with wonder. They were certainly living in the moment, following their hearts, with no real plan. They had courage and adventure in spades. I struggle to recognise myself in that younger woman, and I am saddened to find her almost gone. How I wish I could find just a little part of her energy, her carefree nature, her boldness and take it back.

Ann and I didn't return to Belfast, our lives took us in different directions. I still call Northern Ireland home, my family is there, my roots are deeply woven and from time to time I feel guilty about leaving. Yet I am so grateful to this place – it welcomed me in with arms

Beyond the Sea
Shane Strachan

Summer 1998

This deep, it's ower dark tae mak oot the colours o the baas. The green and blue aa merge intae one like the Caribbean Sea jist ootside the door o the kids' club, beyond the widden deck and white railin.

Yer breath steams up the baas surroondin yer moo and nose, intensifyin the plastic's sweet, sickly scint. The hair on yer heid feels charged wi static, ready tae snap, crackle, pop.

'What are you doing in there?' a voice caas oot fae somewye abeen.

Ye sweem up tae the surface o the baa-pit.

'Don't you wanna draw with the others?' Jenny asks. She looks too bonnie tae be weerin the staff uniform for the Adventurers club: a yalla polo shirt, navy shorts and white plimsolls. She has a perfect American smile, bricht blue een and bleach-blonde hair scrapit back intil a pink scrunchie.

'I'm lookin for the reid and yalla baas,' ye reply.

'The what?'

'The red and yellow balls. I hae tae win the bonus points.'

She covers her moo as she shrieks wi laughter.

'You're the most Scottish person I've ever met, and we meet a lot on these ships!'

Ye shrug and return tae wydin through the baa-pit, randomly howkin up baas in the hope een o them micht be a colour ither than green or blue.

'I dinna think they're in here,' ye say as ye chuck a baa back doon. 'I think you're jist makkin on.'

'I don't have a clue what you're saying, but it's so cute.' She laughs again. 'Come on! Come draw. The best picture gets points too.'

Ye trudge through the pit and lowp oot ower, doon ontae the itchy blue carpet that ay sticks tae yer socks. Jenny pours ye a cup o diluting juice while ye scribble awa at a table wi the ither nine-to-eleven-year-aul Adventurers. Ye tak a sip – it's ower warm and ye can barely mak oot the orange flavour. Ye wish it was caul and fizzy like the drinks they serve bi the pool. Ye've never drank sae much fizzy juice in yer life. This return tae flat juice is a reminder o hame, o sharing a big jug o diluting juice wi yer wee half-brither at suppertime jist a wik afore, back in yer mam's cooncil house in the Broch, thoosands o miles awa.

Een o the ither Adventurers, Justin, sits next tae ye, draawin a picter o his faimly.

He's sketched oot his dad's dark hair, little wee een and a straight line for his moo abeen a reid T-shirt and blue shorts. He leaves the ootline o the face and limbs blank o colour itherwise. In the draawin o his mam, he taks a broon colourin pencil and fills in the ootline o her face, blendin intae the black squiggles o hair. He's draan her wi a big smile that curves up at the edges.

Ye canna mind ever seeing yer mam and dad thigether in a photograph, never mind the same room, so ye decide tae draa yer grandma and granda. They're the eens fa have taen ye on this holiday since you're the peer grand-bairnie fa widna get itherwise.

As ye draa the ootline o yer grandma's stoot body, ye mindlessly and quietly sing alang tae the sang that's playing on the TV in the backgroon – *The Boy is Mine*.

Oot o naewye, a light broon fist thumps ye in the airm and it quickly burns wi a stinging pain.

'Stop singing that song, faggot,' Justin says under his breath.

Yer face starts burnin as much as yer airm. Ye manage tae tak deep breaths until the tears in yer een suck back intae yer heid.

'Okay guys!' Jenny shouts. 'Finish up your pictures because it's time for our family competition out in the basketball court.'

The day afore, you'd went intae Jamaica wi yer grandma tae see the waterfaa in Kingston, so you hae nae idea fit she's on aboot. Suddenly aabody is lined up wi their caps on and you're trailing aifter them, howkin yer T-shirt sleeve doon ower the reid mark on yer airm.

Ye aa mak yer wye oot ontae deck and walk alang the side o the boat towards the basketbaa court at the ither end far a group o dads stand aboot in varying shades o tanned and burnt skin. Justin runs ower tae his dad fa pats him lightly on the shooder. Ye look aroon – yer granda is naewye tae be seen amang the men, and yer grandma isna stood wi the mams congregated ootside the court. Justin's mam is there, standin slightly awa fae the rest o the weemin. Taller than them aa, her dark skin glows in the sunlight.

'Okay guys! Today's family competition is… a… burping competition!' Jenny's vyce booms oot a megaphone.

The dads shak their heads as their bairns jump up and doon cheerin.

Each bairn and dad taks turns tae go up tae the megaphone and try and rift the loudest. Somehoo, each pair manages tae be looder than the last, sometimes even riftin langer as well. Ye try tae work oot hoo their

15

deeing it and notice they seem tae gulp doon air afore forcing it back up oot their swallt bellies. Seen enough, they've aa taen a turn and Jenny looks ower at you, standin on yer ain.

'Do you want to give it a go?'

Aabody turns and stares at ye. Justin smirtles.

Ye nod yer heid and slowly walk ower tae tak the megaphone fae Jenny. Yer airm aches as ye lift it up tae yer moo, yer palms swiytin. Ye tak a deep breath, swallae it doon and then try tae force it back up… A tiny 'ah' comes oot the megaphone. The bairns and their dads burst oot laughin. Justin and his dad piynt at ye as they snicher.

Ye pit the microphone doon and skiyt oot the court. A hand taps at yer shooder as ye start makkin yer wye alang the deck. Ye look up tae see Justin's mam – the sun glares ahin her so that a halo seems tae circle roon her dark curly hair.

'Don't worry about it. That's not a talent anybody should be proud of.'

She rubs at yer airm a wee bit and it taks the sting oot the sair patch a little. She flashes her big smile, and ye gie her a wee een back, afore heidin on tae find yer faimly.

I Don't Like Jelly Babies
Angela McKenna

It was May 1978, and my days in primary school were
ending. Ahead of me lay the promise of languorous
summer months; a sun-drenched, rain-soaked riot
of street games and shared roller-skates, punctuated
occasionally by moments of pleasant boredom. There'd
be no adventures, at least not until the end of the
holidays, when I'd find myself at the 'big school', a place
where the fourth-year lassies would, I was told, plunge
my innocent head into a toilet pan every day. But that
horror was for the future. Until then, it would be just
another normal summer. Or so I thought.

The first sign that something was different came when
my mother arrived home from work one night and
waved a copy of the *Evening Times* under my nose. This
wasn't an attempt to draw my attention to noteworthy
world events, although as the year progressed, we'd
discuss test-tube babies, panic-buying of bread during
the 'Winter of Discontent' and a new soap opera about a
family business in Dallas. Looking back, it all seems so
innocent, but living through it felt exciting – albeit not
as exciting as the article on page 13 of the newspaper. It
took just five words – **Time Lord to Visit City** – to send
me into a paroxysm of joy. I could hardly believe what
I was reading, but there it was in black and white: Tom
Baker would sign books in the Argyle Street branch of
John Menzies on Saturday! The Doctor was coming to
Glasgow, and the world shifted under my feet.

In common with most children of that era, Saturday
teatime meant watching *Doctor Who*, sometimes from

behind the sofa, or at the very least, through splayed fingers. Every episode scared the living daylights out of me. But, no matter how bad it was, I'd be back in my usual place the following week, battling the Daleks and the Cybermen all over again. To say I was obsessed with the show would be an understatement. And my other obsession, reading, soon bled into it, as I slowly amassed a healthy selection of tie-in books to keep me going when the series ended for the year. And here, out of the blue, was an opportunity to get not just another *Doctor Who* book, but one signed by The Doctor himself. I simply *had* to get myself into John Menzies that Saturday morning. Luckily for me, my mother agreed.

And so, after what felt like a year, Saturday finally arrived, and with a pound note tucked into my pocket, I boarded the number 5 bus and headed on my own into the city centre. When the old charabanc finally trundled to a halt in St Enoch's Square, I ran (perish the thought now!) all the way to the shop, arriving purple-faced and breathless, in an instant becoming just one of a thousand excited children, almost all bedecked in *Doctor Who* T-shirts, flared denim and white sandshoes. There was no doubt about it; I was in the right place. Unfortunately, I was also at the end of a very long, snaking queue – but I didn't let it faze me. The Doctor was at the other end of that queue so I was happy to wait.

Time passed pleasantly enough, and before long I was inside the shop where a terrified-looking assistant ushered me through the barrier and down the escalator. I was getting close. In fact, I was getting so close I could hear him. The Doctor's unmistakable voice was now less than twenty feet ahead of me! With little time to spare, and from a conveniently placed table, I chose my book, *Terror of the Zygons*. Then I joined the final line and there were just ten children in front of me. Then it was nine, which quickly became eight, and then... suddenly, it was my turn. As I approached the table, the Time Lordy mass of curls and huge, shiny teeth said, 'Hello, I'm The Doctor. What's your name?' And I said... well, I said nothing, because I froze. Rooted to the spot, I stood, star-struck and unable to speak. To his credit, the man from Gallifrey spotted my predicament, and he took the book from my sweaty hand and signed it. Then he grinned, put his hand in his pocket, and brought out a paper bag, which he held out to me. 'Would you like a Jelly Baby?' he said. From somewhere deep within me I found my voice, and I squeaked out, 'No thank you, I don't like Jelly Babies.' Oh, how he laughed, his guffaws booming across the basement. Then it was time to go, and the hand that wielded the sonic screwdriver every Saturday shook mine, and off I went, shocked and bewildered, having had the time of my life.

The Doctor has changed his face many times since 1978, and I must admit that mine has changed too as the decades have fallen away, one by one. Despite this, I can't help feeling that in the years since my big adventure, time has looped back on itself. Think about it: ABBA came back. Argentina once again won the World Cup. We've just had a summer, autumn and winter of discontent and we've had a pandemic that led to panic-buying of toilet paper instead of bread. Even good old Scotland got to the Euros for yet another glorious failure, although they didn't treat us to a goal like Archie Gemmell's against Holland back in '78. I suppose some things never change. I know I haven't. To this day, I spend many a happy hour having adventures in the TARDIS or with my nose stuck in a book. And funnily enough, I still don't like Jelly Babies.

A Faimlie Tint
Iain Forde

Ae Hogmanay A gaed missin alang wi ma faimlie, ma
dug an ma baudron. We wes mintin ti gae ti fess in
the N'eir wi freins in Diabaig at is in Wester Ross. We
leived in Embro an set aff i the mornin. In thur days it
tuik aw day ti gang norlins sae it wes dirk afoir we cam
ti the heich bit o the rodd abune Loch Morar. Hit wes
rennin sair. The kerr stertit ti skyte about the rodd, sae
A stapped an pit ma haun on the grun. The renn wes
jeillin on the taur an makkin a shete o eiss. Nou, the
rodd wes singil traik an verra narra, hit wes alse gey stey
aw the wey doun ti the loch an gif we hed stertit ti skyte
sydieweys aff the rodd we wuid hae rowed doun the brae
ablo an thon wuid bein the enn o uz. Sae we tirned bak.

Nou we kent at jeillin renn aften menit snaw ti follae.
Thusgates the Slochd summitie suth o Inverness micht
git blokkit an we wuid be stak in thon toun. We cuidna
be shuir o finndin a ottil at wuid tak a dug an a baudron
at Hogmanay, sae we thocht it wyce ti wun owre Slochd
whaur we wuid be sauf frae the snaw. As we gaed by
Achnasheen we sein a fonn buith bot we thocht it wyce
no ti tyne tyme an didna baither fonnin wir freins. Eftir
a bit, we wun owre Slochd an doun bi Speysyde. We wes
nou anhungert an wes stertin ti git laich on peter-uill.
Bot whan we wun ti Carr Brig the anerlie eldrin stance
hed nae peter-uill sae we crowled on til Aviemore whaur
the stance wes steikit up bot the wes a puggie machine
at gied ye eldrin gif ye inpit a fyver. We hed anerlie ane
an pit it in gey releiffit.

Help ma bob, the puggie wuidna tak a Scotch fyver, anerlie ane Inglish nott. Ye maun imaigine the wes a bit sweirin efter thon, bot we juist hed ti cairrie on, gaun verra slaw ti hain wir peter-uill. The tyme passit an ivverrie mament we expekkit the ingyne ti stap. Than the poliss kythit. Thai didna lyk this kerr crowlin alang, pang-fou o fowk in the wie smaw ours sae thai garred uz stap fur rale. Eftir thai hard wir sairie narraution thai proponed at we caw doun ti the poliss-statioun at Kingussie whaur thai wuid gie uz a Inglish fyver fur wir rejekkit Scotch ane an we wull cuid coff eldrin at Newtonmore. This wes whitlik we duin, forleitin at the wuidna be eneuch peter-uill ti wun ti Embro. Than we hed a braw idaia. We wuid gang ti a but an ben at we skaired wi anither faimlie, at liggit nor o Pitlochry.

A kent ma freins wes sauf in Embro an A aye tuik the chak in ma pouch whan A gaed aroun an about. Sae we tirned aff the main rodd an heidit fur the but an ben at wes heich on the hul abune a ferm in a wie glen owre by Loch Tummel. Whyles it wes no possibil ti wun up the brae kiz o the snaw bot we howped at the traik wuid be clair. We wun ti the ferm awricht bot it wes nou that weill throu the nicht at the fowk wes in bed. Sae we laed the kerr an stairtit ti sclim the traik up ti the but an ben. We hed skaired out aw the fuid atwein uz, the dug waukit an wir auldess laddie tuik the baudrons in hiz anorak. Bot whan wi tirned the peth uplins we fand hit wes bot twa furrs o eiss whaur the tractour bene cawin up ti mait the ewes. Ma laddie wes the erest ti skyte owre an he cowped an rowed atap o the baudrons at stak aw hiz cluiks intil'm.

Eftir a bit we wun up ti the but an ben an lichtit the lowes. The wesna onie lectra pouer ye ken, ir rinnin wattir ir a lavvie bot hit wes cosie eneuch. Ma guid wyfe

Dàna-thuras Lallaidh
Seonaidh Charity

Dh'inns ur mac ur sgeulachd dhomh
a bhris an dealbh a bh' agam dhìobh:
am bodach àrd, caol ud le speuclairean cho tiugh,
mar bhuinn nan seann bhotalan Lucozade sin
a bhiodh tu a' caitheamh,
falamh, dhan allt,
aig bonn a' ghàrraidh.

Tha cuimhn' a'm nuair a thabhainn sibh
cnogan Stella orm is mi còig bliadhna deug a dh'aois:
'Siuthad Lofty, cha dèan e cron ort!'
a' priobadh sùil mheudaichte ri m' athair,
ag innse dhuinn mun turas a rinn sibh an latha ud –
a Cheann Loch Biorbhaidh a dh'iarraidh iasg ùr
(cha ghabhadh sibh ach adag)
turas a mhair còrr is sia uairean a thìde,
a' dràibheadh aig trithead mìle san uair.

Ach, sibhse am fear cuideachd, a-rèir aithris,
a bha seòladh raceran air Chluaidh agus air
cuantan meadhan thìreach na Roinn Eorpa is sibh òg,
gleusta, ealanta, ainmeil,
cliùiteach am measg sheòladairean,
grian an t-samhraidh a' dubhadh ghruaidhean bàna
a chaidh àrach air cladaichean garbha
taobh dorch' Loch Bhraoin.

Chuimhnich mi oirbh san t-seann chathair
san t-seòmar-suidhe latha foghair,
is dh'fhairich mi air mo ghruaidh
oiteag bheag gaoithe bhlàth
nan cuantan cèine.

Lallie's Adventure

Your son told me a story today
that shattered the image I had of you:
the tall, slim bodach with thick-lensed glasses
like the bottoms of those old Lucozade bottles
you dumped in the burn
at the foot of the garden.

I remember when you offered me
a can of Stella when I was fifteen years old:
'On yoursel' Lofty, it won't do you any harm!'
a magnified eye winking at my father,
then recounting the tale of your recent adventure north –
Kinlochbervie in search of fresh fish
(you'd only eat haddock)
a trip that took a full day,
since you drove at thirty miles an hour.

But, you were also the man, apparently,
who raced yachts on the Clyde and on the
Mediterranean when you were a lad,
skilled, expert, sought-after,
famous among sailors,
the summer sun darkening the pale cheeks,
raised on the rocky shores
on the dark side of Lochbroom.

I remembered you in your old armchair
in your living-room on an autumn afternoon,
and felt on my cheek
a warm gentle breeze
from faraway shores.

Share your love of books...

Scottish Book Trust is an independent national charity. Our mission is to ensure people living in Scotland have equal access to books.

If you're enjoying this book, please consider making a donation so that everyone in Scotland has the opportunity to improve their life chances through books and the fundamental skills of reading and writing.

Visit **scottishbooktrust.com/donate** to find out more.

Answering the call

The Reluctant Adventurer
Taslin Pollock

'How deep is it?' I ask the man over the phone.

'Not that deep,' he replies. 'Besides, you'll have a life jacket on. Go on. You can't be the only one watching from the sidelines.'

'Alright. I'll do it,' I say, the man's positivity contagious. For a brief moment, I feel euphoric about saying yes. As soon as I hang up, a pang of nausea washes over me. Why on earth did I just agree to go paddleboarding in a murky canal in Falkirk? I don't do stuff like this. When I applied for life insurance a few years back, the lady on the phone asked me whether I snowboarded or went skydiving. Pretty much every adventurous pursuit you could think of, she asked me about. I answered 'no' to every single question and at the end of the call, I couldn't help but be struck by how boring my life is. I like being boring. I'm the one who comes across things like paddleboarding at the Falkirk Wheel on the internet and signs up my husband and children, and I watch from the sidelines, snapping pictures on my phone. That's the way I like it. So whatever possessed me to say yes?

Maybe because, like everyone else, I'd spent the last few years not being able to do anything like this, or maybe it was because the man on the phone was a very good salesman. Definitely the latter. I wonder whether to call up and tell him I've changed my mind. I wait until dinner to tell my family what I've done. My husband laughs, my eldest joins in and my youngest tries hard to tell me she thinks it's awesome I'm joining them. When I complain about not having old shoes I am happy to lose to the canal, everyone laughs harder. I wish I'd not told them.

The paddleboarding is booked for the next day, not enough time for me to think about wishing for apocalyptic floods, but still plenty of time hoping to get a call to tell me it's cancelled. My phone doesn't ring.

I get up early the next day. It's dry. Light jacket weather. Not roasting and not baltic and, in Scotland, that's pretty much a win. I wear my swimming costume under my clothes, pack towels, underwear, old shoes for everyone else but me and water bottles and change for the car park. When we get there it's still early. There are a few people milling about and a narrowboat coming into a lock. I see the man standing waiting at the paddleboard station. He looks like one of those old fishermen you see on the boats at the harbour towns. His face still shows signs of a tan he must have got on the only sunny day of the year so far.

'I'm Geoff. I'll be your paddleboard instructor. Just change into your swimming costumes and I'll get you all set up with life jackets and boards,' he tells us.

'Err, sorry what? I thought we got wetsuits. I'm fairly certain that there were people wearing wetsuits in the pictures I saw on social media,' I panic. Being adventurous is one thing, wearing just my swimming costume on the Grand Union Canal for the whole of Falkirk to see… well, that's something else entirely. I wish I'd shaved my legs now.

'I'll just go and check with my colleagues,' Geoff says, scarpering.

'There's no way I'm doing it in just my costume,' I hiss through my gritted teeth.

'You're right. Wetsuits are this way,' Geoff says.

'Great,' I reply, without any enthusiasm.

Geoff hands us all wetsuits, 'That should be alright for you.' He hands me a faded blue wetsuit with tattered sleeves that still feels damp.

It's like wearing tights all over your body. Trying to put it on while also sharing a small cubicle with your smallest child and trying not to flail an arm or make strange noises is no mean feat, and I'm not even in the water.

We all waddle back over to the paddleboarding station, where Geoff is waiting to fit us up with life jackets. He puts a child's life jacket over my body and tightens it. My chest is now much flatter.

Geoff gives us the safety briefing and an introduction to paddleboarding.

'Can you do the whole lesson without falling in?' I ask as I am about to step onto the paddleboard.

'It's possible,' Geoff says. I cling onto that.

The paddleboard is larger than I thought it would be, which I'm glad about. I kneel on the board, and I start rowing, trying to remember Geoff's instructions. I manage to grasp paddling forward, stopping is trickier and turning around takes a fair few goes to get right. Did I end up in the bank of the canal stuck between the reeds? Almost certainly. Did I ignore pleas of help from my youngest, who it turns out isn't good at this? Probably. Geoff helped her. Did I refuse to stand up on my board? Maybe. Did I stay dry? Yes, I bloody did.

I loved it. Even though my arms ached and my tummy muscles complained, the whole thing felt exhilarating. I felt like Pocahontas, albeit in a less glamorous get-up and colder climate. The canal is a wondrous place, dark misty waters under my oar but surrounded by the beauty of the wildflowers. The frequent cyclists and pedestrians who always said hello. The best thing was finally doing an activity with my family for a change. Together. There are obviously no photos, so you'll just have to take my word for it, but I am braver than I realise. Saying yes gave me an experience no one can take away.

Author note: *This story is based on a true story when the man over the phone convinced me to try paddleboarding at the Falkirk Wheel with my family.*

Once Upon an Awkward Time
Len Pennie

Once upon an awkward time
In a kingdom close to here,
Lived a princess much inclined,
to face her greatest fear

Though she had ruled her kingdom with the greatest
    of propriety
Her noble quest, the toughest test: to overcome anxiety

Things that cause her palms to sweat and tightly force to
    clench her
Jaw are things that barely count as having an adventure

Slaying dragons can't compare with ordering a drink
Poison apples don't come close to how she'd overthink
When phoning up the doctor, it's just far too great an ask
Making awkward small talk is a herculean task

So she enlisted help from someone trained who could
    assist,
Not a fairy, witch or godmother but licensed therapist,
Who told her she was normal and all hope was far from
    dead,
That mental illness is a curse that lives inside the head

I'm getting fairly meta though by this point it should be,
Fairly obvious to all that the princess here is me,
I tend to use my poetry and convoluted prose,

To communicate the way I feel so everybody knows,
Mental illness isn't something I will ever fix,
But with some medication and a host of clever tricks,
I'm far more able to exist and be unsymptomatic,
My life's not quite a fairytale, but it's now much less
  dramatic.

The Journey to ABE
Malcolm Johnston

On Monday morning I woke up and got changed to go out the door to catch the number 35 bus to take me to the bus station. I walked across the road and I came to a big building, grey with green copper decoration. It looks a bit scary and a bit austere. But it's a building where adult learning takes place, known locally as 'The Kremlin'!

I walk up the steps and am faced with two brown doors. I press the door buzzer – it says ABE, this is Adult Basic Education and where I go for my two classes. Give her a few minutes and here comes Sarah, my tutor, to answer the door. She's always nice and happy and her eyes are always sparkling.

It's time for my creative writing class. I wonder who is here today in the group. I wonder what we are doing today. It's something I've never heard of before. It's called acrostic poems. I feel weird and nervous because I don't know what it means but once we talk about it and see some examples I feel better. I know I can do it.

So, I write the word 'Scotland' down the side of the paper and then for each letter I make up a sentence about Scotland. So, for the letter 'S', I write, 'Scotland has a great view of thistles and mountains and lochs'. I get into the swing of it and I actually enjoy it. I finish first. Everyone listens to my acrostic poem. I feel proud.

We stop for a coffee and listen to other people's poems. Everybody's poems are great. It's now 12.30pm and time to finish. It's been a good morning and I enjoyed the class. Now it's time to go home. It's been a great adventure taking part in this group and being listened to. I head for the bus station and wonder what we will be doing next Monday – a new adventure.

Author note: *It's been a big deal for me to come to adult learning classes and I feel it's an adventure which I am on.*

Adventure Girl
Kirsty Niven

Stumbling through sienna woods,
the branches tickle my face
in dried, papery coils – autumn leaves ready
to dive to the ground like lemmings.

I can't see the path behind me,
can only faintly hear the dog's bark
and the rustle of the picnic bag.
Gretel's breadcrumbs forgotten.

Pine needles sneak into the holes
of my worn-out Converse,
shaking up and down with each step
like the sands of an hourglass.

I was always told I wasn't enough,
too cowardly, too boring.
I had to adopt an alter ego:
Adventure Girl, the superhero.

I can see her running on ahead of me,
infinitely perfect and confident.
A mountain goat climbing every rock;
everything a competition, a show.

I blink her fiction away so easily.
Façades dropped in this solitude,
I'm swallowed up by the enormity
of a forest that doesn't care who's brave.

A Sort-of Father Christmas
L Philipp Naughton

I moved from my job in Shetland to Italy, with my wife,
a daughter of five and a son of three, in 1998. Not much
difference between the two really; a little bit more
sunshine, a few less windy days, a few more trees – and
a lot less sheep! I loved my time in Shetland. It was a big
leap, having not even seen the place I was going to be
working in until the plane touched down in Bari. I had
one weekend and a single day at work with the person I
was replacing. I was on my own for four months before
my family moved out to join me, with my knowledge
of Italy consisting of two holidays and the most basic
'una pizza per favore'. This was the rural south, 'il
mezzogiorno' (half-day) in a town of 26,000 far removed
from the slick holiday adverts of the 'cultured north'.

Let's roll on a few years. Both children were in Italian
state schools and my grasp of Italian, fortunately, was
vastly improved. It had to be. I was working and living
amongst many who couldn't speak English and there
were adventures aplenty. One day I was in the workshop
with the twenty regular Italians, although my job also
entailed frequent contact with many more. Suddenly, they
slowly formed a standing semi-circle as the bay manager
sat on a chair in the middle. This had to be big. By now all
conversations were in Italian. He leant forward.

'Lorenzo, you know Babbo Natale?'

'Uhm,' I was thinking, 'should I?'

'Personally?' I asked. That caused confusion.

'Babbo Natale. How do you say, er, Father Christmas.'

'Haven't spoken to him for a while.' Luckily they knew my sense of humour. Not a twitch of any mouth or the raise of any eyebrow. This had to be really big.

'We want you to be Babbo Natale.'

'Uhm, er, OK.'

'Just like that?'

'Yes.'

The cheers would have put Serie A supporters to shame. I thought for a moment that there was going to be popping of prosecco corks. It transpired that I had volunteered to be Babbo Natale for the base's Christmas party, the biggest and most prestigious event of the year.

Next came what Babbo Natale had to say. I'd done quite a lot of acting. There are only three words, well, one word spoken three times.

The base manager and his chosen specialists began the next day.

'Ho-ho-ho.' Said with gusto. The 'h' in Italian is always silent.

'No Lorenzo, o-o-o.' (Pronounced a bit like the 'o' in 'hob'.)

'O-o-o.'

'Louder.'

'O-O-O.'

'Sounds like you are in pain.'

'O-o-o.'

'Now you sound French.'

Three days of despair before the moment of joy.
One month passed. I had the outfit, the tickly beard and the oversized boots. My daughter told our friends downstairs that Father Christmas was visiting our flat almost every day and was rewarded with a sympathetic pat on the head.

I had been chosen, apparently, because my Italian

was good enough to cope with several hundred Italian children but the accent meant that I clearly wasn't local and so would be much more believable.

Four days to go.

Babbo Natale arrives in a sleigh – doesn't he? – and Italian hangars don't have chimneys.

'You do know Babbo Natale will be arriving in the back of a Tornado bomber, don't you?'

'I do now!'

The plan sounded easy. Hangar doors shut. Tornado bomber in place. Engines on, revved up to sound like the plane is landing and the commentator inside the hangar giving it maxi excitement. The engines wind down, the cockpit is opened at the same time as the hangar doors and the adoring throng see Babbo Natale climb down with his sack. It's game on and all is well.

Tornado bomber aircrew are lean, mean fighting machines, fitter than most of us can imagine and most definitely slimmer than me with two enormous cushions held in place with Velcro straps. Part of the tradition is also throwing sweets for the children, hence pockets stuffed full with about four kilos-worth. I defy anyone to do it gracefully. My stomach, fortunately, did not become detached but there was a distinct sideways slew that looked in need of an immediate, life-saving operation. Step two, the wave, followed by a steady Father Christmas swagger down the gantry. We're talking three metres high here, and the next problem. The cushions meant I couldn't see my feet and the boots were not the ones I normally wore. They had no grip. Unsteady, sack flailing and swaying, I somehow made it. Probably some of the parents were cringing inwardly at the thought of Babbo Natale having had one too many grappas on his journey!

The hangar doors opened ever wider. The horde of over-excited children, fuelled by expectation and far too much ice cream and cake, were ready to stampede. And then it happened! Cool outside air met warm inside air. My glasses fogged in seconds and I could see absolutely nothing.

'Babbo Natale, caramelle, caramelle.' It was sweet-throwing time. I'd been reliably told to throw them far and wide so all the children had a chance to pick them up. Quite blind, I imagined a scene reminiscent of pigeons being fed. I flung the sweets in every direction, in as big clumps as my mittens would allow. One salvo struck a woman nearby, who used language that Babbo Natale should never, ever hear.

It calmed down. All I had to do now was sit the children on my knee. The first one was a little girl and her present, twice her size, was deposited next to me. It's an Italian thing. She screamed, the mother looked like I was committing murder. The father told his daughter that I was nice and the parents started arguing.

Shakespeare was in the crowd. All's well that ends well, and fortunately the rest of the evening did.

Author note: *Being asked by the Italian Air Force at a base in southern Italy to be their Father Christmas. I didn't realise until afterwards that it was considered to be a huge honour and responsibility and they were surprised, to say the least, by how quickly I'd agreed to it.*

Adventure's End
Stacie Munro

It rained the day they closed the libraries for good.
The death had been swift in the end;
a shock diagnosis, a whimpering fight,
acceptance.
For weeks they came, faces sombre, choking upon
  condolences as they
mumbled their outrage that those buildings
those places
would soon be stripped away forever.
Children clutching at hands, embarrassed to be kind,
  offered
farewell cards from behind their fathers' backs,
their militant mothers staring down the television
  cameras
and newspapermen,
determined to fight to the end.
Some went quietly,
those familiar wrinkled faces who slipped away without
  fanfare.
Others banged each drum loudly as
the doors were hammered shut.
Some wept when their adventures ended,
those familiar paper portals closed to them
for good.
The death had been swift in the end,
and it rained that day regardless.

Author note: *A poem about the sudden closure of
libraries, and those who rallied against it.*

Mullach Mont Blanc
Alistair Paul

Mar bu ghnàth dhi, bha Ciorstaidh aig a h-obair tràth
mus tàinig a' chòrr de luchd-obrach an supermarket dhan
robh i na manaidsear a-steach, agus i fhathast dorcha.
Cho luath 's a neo-ghlais i doras na h-aitreibh bha fhios
aice gur e madainn dhùbhlanach a bha gu bhith roimhpe.
Shlaighd an dà dhoras fèin-ghluasadach fosgailte mar
bu chòir, ach cha do shlaighd ach aonan dhiubh air ais
na àite na dèidh, a' ciallachadh gum biodh rag-ghèile
a' sèideadh tro na h-aisles le gach oiteig a-muigh gus
an tigeadh an dealanair, nam faigheadh i grèim air fear
idir ann. Bhiodh gearanan ann agus cò dhan tigeadh
na gearanan sin? Cò ach Ciorstaidh Nic an Tàilleir. Gus
chùisean a dhèanamh na bu mhiosa, dh'aithnich i air
an fhuaraidheachd a shuain i nach robh an goileadair
teasachaidh ag obair mar bu chòir; a-rithist. A-rithist,
dhìrich i an staidhir chumhang a lean suas dhan lobhta
far an do thàmh a' bhiast chaochlaideach ann an oisinn
doilleir. Le cniadachadh air a h-uidheam-smachd is faclan
brosnachail, bha an tinneal air dùsgadh mu dheireadh
thall le srann. Air dhi teàrnadh dhan stòr-lann, chuir
i fòn dhan roinn chàraidh. Seadh, seadh, bha iad air
a' chùis a chlàradh. Bhiodh innleadair an làthair san
aithghearrachd; an aon duan a bha air a bhith aca fad
grunn sheachdainean a-nis.

    Thog Ciorstaidh a sùil bhon fhòn aice, a' toirt a-steach
am mì-rian ceithir thimcheall oirre. Bha na cèidsichean-
troilidh air an sgapadh mun làir mar dhannsairean
craicte a bha air an luchd a sgeitheadh asta mus robh

iad air reothadh. Bha an t-aiseag dhan eilean air a bhith anmoch an latha roimhe is, a rèir choltais, cha deach aig sgioba na hoidhch' araoir air an stuth a thàinig a-steach oirre a rèiteachadh. Rud a dh'adhbharachadh tuilleadh ghearanan mu sgeilpichean bàna. 'Sin an treas turas taobh a-staigh cola-deug nach eil bainne Cravendale air a bhith agaibh, is e an aon seòrsa a thèid agam air òl. Na h-allergies agam, fhios agaibh.' Chluinneadh i mar-tha na guthan na ceann.

Mu dheireadh, mu dheireadh, nas fhaide air a' mhadainn, chaidh aice air snàigeadh air falbh bho ghearanan chustamairean is cheistean à luchd-obrach, is fhuair i a-steach dhan oifis aice far an cuireadh i aghaidh air cunntasan is clàran-obrach. Bha Sìne, an leas-mhanaidsear, mar-tha na suidhe aig a deasg, cupa cofaidh na boisean, plìonas air a haodann. Bha aighear na tè ud an co-rèir gainnead a cuid teòmachd. Bha i dìreach a' dèanamh suidhe nuair a sheirm am fòn air a deasg.

'Am faigh thu sin, a Shìne?' thuirt i.

Thàinig Sìne a-null dhan deasg aig Ciorstaidh, stùirc oirre is thog i am fòn. Thàinig bìgeil fhann bhon labhrair.

'Arthur Semple. Tha e airson bruidhinn riut.' Bha coltas buadhail oirre nuair a shìn Sìne am fòn gu Ciorstaidh.

'Arthur, ciamar a tha sibh?' bhruidhinn Ciorstaidh a-steach dhan inneal. 'Dè a tha a dhìth oirbh an-diugh?'

Bu chòir gun cuireadh luchd-ceannaich na h-òrduighean aca a-steach air-loidhne, ach cha robh dòigh air thalamh gun dèanadh fear a rugadh fada mus robh sgeul air an eadar-lìon a' chùis air sin. Bha Ciorstaidh air a h-àireamh a thoirt seachad dhàsan is do dhòrlach de dhaoine eile a bha san aon shuidheachadh gus an cuireadh iad na h-òrduighean aca asteach air a' fòn.

'Dìreach na chumas mi an taobh sa dhen uaigh.'

Thàinig gròcail tron loidhne. An sùil a hinntinn chitheadh Ciorstaidh an fhàrdach dhìblidh san robh an truaghan a' tighinn beò, taobh thall na loidhne, taobh thall an eilein. Soithichean salach air an càrnadh sa mhias, seann phàipearan-naidheachd sgaoilte timcheall air mar gun deach an ruagadh tron t-seòmar leis a' ghaoith, an cat robach, aosmhor aige suas is sìos air clàran-obrach a' chidsin is a' bhòrd-bìdh. Air a bheulaibh, an teilidh aige, a chluinneadh i air cùl guth an duine, 's e a' seirm dhan t-saoghal, a' cumail cuideachd leis. An aon chuideachd a gheibheadh e taobh a-muigh a' chairteal na h-uarach a bhiodh an cùramaiche aige a-staigh.

'Briosgaidean, tha fhios agad air an t-seòrsa is fheàrr leam, aran, bainne.' Gu h-obann gheàrr Arthur a-steach air fhèin. 'Tha rudeigin agam ri innse dhut. Feumar innse do chuideigin agus 's tusa i.' Bu chòir do Ciorstaidh greasad a chur air an duine, ach cha b' urrainn dhi. Shuidh i air ais san t-sèithir aice. 'A Shìne, am faigh thu cupa cofaidh dhomh?' thuirt i ris a co-obraiche, a shiolp air falbh na thòir gu diombach.

Chuir i làn a h-aire air a' fòn na làimh. 'Niste, Arthur, leanaibh oirbh.'

'Ceathrad bliadhna bhon diugh fhèin.' Bha an guth aig Arthur fann, fad às, mar gun robh e gu dearbh a' tighinn thuice thar ceathrad bliadhna ceòthach de thìm. 'Bha mi air Mullach Mont Blanc. Ràinig sinn e sa chamhanaich, fhios agad, às dèidh dhuinn an refuge fhàgail san dorchadas. Bu sinn fhèin a' chiad rud air an do bhuail a' ghrian. Fada shìos fodhainn, bha na bailtean fhathast san dorchadas is na solasan aca a' priobadh oirnn mar reultan, mar gun deach an saoghal bun os cionn. Dh'fhairich mi mar dhia an latha ud, am fianais cruitheachd an domhain. Bha mi nas beò an uair sin na riamh roimhe no riamh bhuaithe.'

46

Lean sàmhchair fhada, san do sheas Ciorstaidh
is Arthur air Mullach Mont Blanc, taobh ri taobh,
a' coimhead sìos air latha air ùr-bhreith gus, mu
dheireadh, chuir Arthur crìoch air òrdugh.

Nuair a thill Ciorstaidh dhan bhùth shìos an ceann
beagan ùine, bhuail oiteag Artach oirre tron doras leth-
fhosgailte. Fa chomhair bu lèir dhi an dithis newstart òg
aice is iad a' siabadh mu na sgeilpichean mar chearcan
gun chinn. Bho oir a sùla mhothaich i do chustamair
a bha a' dèanamh oirre le sgoinn. Gu h-iongantach,
fhuair i nach robh dad dhe seo ga cur suas no sìos. Cha
robh anns na rudan buaireasach sin ach solasan fann
a' priobadh oirre aig astar is i na seasamh air mullach
beinne.

The Summit of Mont Blanc

As usual, Kirsty was at her work early. It was still
dark when she rummaged in her pocket, fished out a
clump of keys and activated the sliding doors into the
supermarket of which she was the manager. The doors
whirred ponderously open. Only one closed behind her.
It was then she knew it was going to be one of those
mornings. Until an electrician came, if she could even
get hold of one, an Arctic wind would blow up and down
the aisles with every flurry of wind outside. There would
be complaints. And who would those complaints come
to? Who but Kirsty Taylor. To make matters worse, as
soon as she stepped into the store and found herself
enveloped in cold, dank air, she knew the heating boiler
was not working; again. Again, she climbed the steep,
narrow stair that led from the warehouse up into the

loft where the slumbering beast dwelt in a dark corner. She caressed its controls and whispered encouraging words to it until eventually it awoke with a sonorous hum. Returning to the warehouse she phoned the maintenance department. Yes, yes, they had recorded the problem. An engineer would visit soon. The same response she had been getting for weeks now.

Lifting her eyes from her phone Kirsty took in the confusion surrounding her. The trolley cages were scattered round her like crazy dancers who had spewed out their contents across the floor before freezing on the spot. The last ferry to the island had been late the day before and the night shift had apparently failed to get all the goods that had come across on her out on the shelves before scarpering. More complaints. About empty shelves this time. 'That is the third time inside a fortnight you have had no Cravendale milk. It's the only kind I can drink, you know. It's my allergies.' She could already hear the voices in her head.

Eventually, eventually, later that morning she managed to steal away from customer complaints and the questioning of her staff and retreat to her office, where she would confront her accounts and staff rotas. Jean, the deputy manager, was already at her desk, a cup of coffee cradled in her palms, a vacant smile on her face. The woman's capacity for cheerfulness was in inverse proportion to her ability. Kirsty had just sat down at her desk when the phone rang.

'Will you get that, Jean?' she said.

Jean drifted reluctantly across to Kirsty's desk. There came a faint squeaking from the speaker.

'It's Arthur Semple. It's you he wants to speak to.' With a triumphant look Jean handed the phone back to Kirsty.

'Arthur, how are you today?' Kirsty's good-humoured

voice gave no hint of her simmering vexation when she spoke into the phone. 'What do you need today?'

By rights customers would put in their orders for home delivery online. Of course, there was no way that someone like Arthur, who was born long before the internet was even dreamt of, would cope with that. Kirsty had given her direct line to him and a handful of others in the same situation so that they could phone their orders in.

'Not much. Just enough to keep me this side of the grave,' came Arthur's croaky reply. In her mind's eye Kirsty visualised the man's wretched home at the other end of the line. Dirty dishes piled in the sink, old newspapers scattered round him as if a whirlwind had ripped through the room. His old cat up and down on the kitchen table and worktops. In front of him the telly which she could hear in the background blaring out, his only company outside the half an hour that his carer would be in, or the five minutes or so it would take him to phone in his food order every couple of days.

'Biscuits, you know the type I like, bread, milk.' Suddenly Arthur cut in on himself. 'I have something to tell you. I need to tell someone.' She should have cut him short, told him she didn't have time. But she couldn't. She sat back in her chair. 'Jean, will you get me a coffee?' she said to her colleague, her hand over the mouthpiece. Jean sloped off as if she was dragging a heavy load.

Kirsty gave her full attention to the phone.

'You were saying, Arthur.'

'Forty years ago, from this very day.' Arthur's voice was faint, as if it was indeed coming to her across forty misty years of time. 'I was on the summit of Mont Blanc. We arrived at dawn. It was dark when we left the refuge. We were the very first thing to be lit by the sun that day. Far below us the villages were still in darkness. Their lights glimmered like stars, as if the whole world had turned upside down. I felt like a god witnessing the creation of the universe. I was more alive that day than ever before, or ever since.'

There followed a long silence in which Arthur and Kirsty stood side by side on the summit of Mont Blanc looking down on the birth of a new day until, after some time, Arthur finished his order.

When Kirsty returned to the shop floor towards lunchtime she was struck by an icy wind sweeping through the half-open doors. In front of her two new-starts were drifting aimlessly round the shelves like headless chickens. At a distance she could make out a customer heading in her direction with great intent. Strangely, she felt calm. All these irritations heaped upon her were only as faint lights blinking at her as she stood resolutely on her summit looking down on them from a distance.

Rue
Mae Diansangu

Wir bodies are stories.

Hers is freshly scrieved.
Saft an swak wi newness.

Mine's a bitty teuch, wi a
'bin aroon the block'-ness.

She is easier tae read.

Nae secret self swirlin roon her
een. Insteid, some fierdy wards

set in amber: nivver hud ontae
a moment langer than it lasts.

I waatch her filter the warld
through that wee broon neb.

Ahin a nuvelty. Ivry olfactory
receptor a hame fur opportunity.

A curious tongue keeks oot,
slaikin ower fresh possibilities.

The wye her body meets ilka
day,   hiz   learnt   me   tae

slow

                doon

an

                sniff oot

adventure

                                in

                the maist

familiar

                corners.

So we tak wir bodies an wir stories
fur a wak. An we mak the warld

mair whole an newer. A callerness
sets ower the auldest routes I ken.

We traik them, again an again.
Blithe, glaikit, and content

tae spy summin new
in ivry sauchelt neuk.

Metal Detecting
Callum McCormack

In farmers' fields, ploughed and tilled and crops sown for hundreds of years, we searched endlessly for a legendary hoard of Roman gold coins.

But between cling-film-wrapped sandwiches, Grampa would turn to me, empty-handed, and say, 'We'll try the field over next time. We'll have better luck there.' I already felt lucky.

When you're of a certain age, it's easy to find adventure in everything. When you are smaller, every step feels half as long. Imagination runs wild: beds become race cars, discarded boxes become rocket ships heading to far-off lands. Your heroes take on near-mythical form.

Growing up, adventure took the form of long walks in the countryside around the town where I lived, and still do. Always in my Grampa's company.

We would set off from my parents' house in knitted woollen jumpers courtesy of my gran, with a metal detector slung over his shoulder. When he took a step, I'd need a step and a half to keep up. Our spot wasn't far, you'd be lucky if it was half a mile from the front door, but it felt like a different world. We would spend the route march talking about what he'd been reading, or about what we were going to find.

He had consulted the maps, read the books. It was a sure thing. There had to be something beneath the soil around here. They'd found Roman coins just a few miles away. Why would they stop there?

But time after time we'd return to the same spots and unearth the same treasures. Rarely more than a few belt buckles and bottle tops. The only time a coin turned up was a 1966 sixpence found at the bottom of the field. Just my luck.

Then it was on to the next adventure, out of the field and heading towards the old farmhouse that must once have stood proud at the head of the field. Time had taken its toll. The roof was mostly bare of shingles and the first floor had grown weary of its place and now almost lay behind the front door, as if the house was saying it had had its fill of visitors and was trying to keep the outside world at arm's length.

But where there's a will there's a way, and we found a way inside. Through windows that had long given up the ghost and were now paneless. There was something voyeuristic about being in there, exploring each room that hadn't succumbed to time over and over again. Wondering what had happened in the years that it had been inhabited.

This was once a family home. It was easy to allow your thoughts to wander, to imagine what it was like for the people who had spent their days here. A farmer waking up before the birds, pushing tired feet into heavy work boots in a chair that faced a TV that he fell asleep in front of at night before he had the chance to watch it. A wife who laid towering plates of food on the table, enough to keep him strong. Kids just like me running around dreaming of when all this would be theirs.

It's easy to be idealistic and anachronistic when you have a blank canvas like that.

No mobile phones in those days. My parents would begin to worry about where I was. Which far-flung land had we found ourselves in this time? But eventually, often well after dinner had been served and plates cleared, I would collapse in through the door, exhausted. At night, from my bedroom window, I could look between the trees and the Levi's factory at the bottom of my road and just about make out where we had been.

Where we once spent afternoons snaking up and down the fields, digging, sifting, patting empty soil back into place, modernisation has taken over. About ten years ago, an oil company built a factory on the spot where I found the sixpence. The dilapidated farmhouse is now a petrol station. It would be poignant, although perhaps a little sad, to say that when they dug the land up they unearthed what we'd been looking for, but they didn't find anything either. It might be better for that bit of treasure to stay elusive. Sometimes the hope can be what kills you, but sometimes it is the hope that drives you.

As we both grew older, the frequency of the walks slowed. After a handful of heart attacks, they had all but ceased for Grampa but he kept doing the reading, kept consulting the maps. Eventually I reached my teenage years and other interests took over. There's no treasure in regret, but I will admit that, as time has passed, I have grown to wish I had spent more time walking.

But you always think one day you'll get back to it. You still hope adventure will emerge from the mist like Brigadoon. One day something will spark within you and you'll have the thought to wonder what could be over there in that unexplored corner of your world.

When he died, as a family we descended on his old flat to do what had to be done. I looked through drawers and cupboards, once again looking for treasures. In a red biscuit tin, I found the same old treasures, belt buckles, bottle tops. This time though, they were much more valuable.

Treasures Fae the Ebb
Ingrid Grieve

Bits o driftwid
bonny stones
sea gless green and blue
shells aal shapes and colours
a grottie buckie too

a bottle top
a seabird's skull
a rusty owld padlock
a piece o Sunday china
wedged atween the rocks

a scarriman's heid
in shellmaleens
o purple pink and blue
waashed up ware o reds, greens, golds,
a myriad o hues

a selkie's heid
abune the waves
ancient folklore eyes
a glisk o light
oot in the haaf
fae a glettan late voar sky

whitemas, kittos
malliemacks
glide kithy winds wae glee
singan high-pitched seasalt shanties
tae the bass runge o the sea

the whisper
o the marram
as it dances on the dune
the seaspray scatter on the rock
the gouster's whistlan tune

the crashan waves
the shore birds' song
the wind percussion sand
a cacophony o music
fae the shoreside skiffle band

Author note: *Living in Orkney means we're never far from the sea. This poem is inspired by many walks along the shore.*

Quest
Lynn Blair

Not there. But here, now. . .

Lie on cold ground, watch the insects move, and the
wind dance a dizzy with long grass. Follow the woodlice
and discover their home. There's a world of
intrigue under that flowerpot.

Let today be different.

At dawn, go outside, watch the clouds drift over,
majestic forms on a slow push to elsewhere. Care for
one. Place your mind in the folds of its cloak and drift
a bit, upwards, outwards. The drone of rush hour be
damned. You're here. Here. Put an ear to the earth
and listen to its depth. Fill your mind with roots.
Things will tilt and shift. Your ground.

. . . is where you can find good things.

You don't need a bucket list, twenty destinations,
or a death wish.

Instead: walk barefoot on cold grass, in snow, on ice and
remind yourself you're wild. Stand in the rainstorm and
listen to the beat, pat, pat, of the droplets. Move. There
are books in that library you've never read, whole worlds
and characters paused there, awaiting the browse of
your mind. Swim in the sea but be still awhile; part of

the waves and the strangeness of salt. Later, you'll tuck
in your mer-tail (others might find it distracting) but it
won't stop you climbing a tree and sitting awhile unseen,
a witness to the leaves. Turn the wrong way out the
station. Choose the ugly place and look for a diamond.
It's right there, right here, all around you. Leave others
to their choices. Adventure is found in your quest to
make the most of a rainy Monday, a week with an empty
wallet, a day when everything goes wrong. You know
how this life is. You know how it goes. How quickly.

After dark, lie with a blanket under the stars,
conducting a symphony of satellites. Regret nothing.
Tend the small spaces. Touch what's not inviting.
Be grateful. Seek.

Deep days, wide and full.

Author note: *I don't consider myself an adventurous
person at all, but I do always try to look for the magic
in the everyday.*

Share your love of books...

Scottish Book Trust is an independent national charity. Our mission is to ensure people living in Scotland have equal access to books.

If you're enjoying this book, please consider making a donation so that everyone in Scotland has the opportunity to improve their life chances through books and the fundamental skills of reading and writing.

Visit **scottishbooktrust.com/donate** to find out more.

So Many Ordinary Women
Gill Ryan

Despite our best efforts, we couldn't locate a map of the
Fife Witches Trail, so we set off without one, trusting
local knowledge to keep us right. All we had were the
names of three villages whose infamy lies in their
history of killing women accused of witchcraft during
Scotland's dark times. Torryburn, Valleyfield, Culross.
If we were expecting the haunted guilt of a Salem-type
community, what we got was three picturesque coastal
towns peopled by the friendliest of folk.

The Torryburn car park had information boards,
but no mention of the Witches Trail. We wandered
through the village asking people along the way. No one
seemed to be quite sure what we meant. Not a shifty
denial of the village's dark past, but a genuine look of
bemusement when we mentioned a plaque. A kind
cyclist went out of her way to get directions and told
us to look near the bridge. Another directed us along a
woodland path in the opposite direction, towards the
Witches Tower. Like a Choose-Your-Own-Adventure
story where you keep a finger in the book to return to
the other option, we picked both.

The trail through the woods became progressively
eerier until we found ourselves surrounded by hundreds-
of-years-old yew trees bent into wonderfully weird
shapes. One looked like draped limbs, crossing its legs and
leaning in for a blether. Another was apparently weeping
blood; the coagulated red sap and the cleft in the trunk it
flowed from looked like a menstruating vulva.

The victims of the Scottish witch trials of the seventeenth to eighteenth centuries were ordinary folk; wifies who knew herbal remedies, brewers, powerless servant girls, widows who owned land, pious women (and men) shocked to be named by others under torture. It's unlikely any of them considered themselves a witch. Had there been actual witches though, this yew grove felt like a mystical space they'd have met in. Next to it, the Witches Tower, a large private house built over the remains of a seventeenth-century one, was a let-down.

As we headed back along the coastal path, what we thought was the Witch's Rock, where women accused of witchcraft were tried by drowning, was visible out in the bay. Seeming to be accessible at low tide, we risked wading out across the outwardly firm mudflats, using seaweed as handholds. We abandoned our foolishness when the mud tried to steal our boots and locals on the coastal path stopped to look out at us with concern. The tide can come in rapidly on this small bay on the Firth of Forth. Anyway, as we discovered later, it was the wrong rock.

Back on shore, we met a more knowledgeable local couple and discovered that the nameless bust on a plinth near the car park is Lillias Adie, the only 'witch' to have a known grave. Accused of fornicating with the devil, Lillias refused to name others under torture and died before she could be executed. With luck the couple could point out her intertidal grave, only accessible at low tide, which was still in our favour. A solid, thick, maybe metre-long sandstone slab with no obvious markings was placed over her grave, to prevent the devil from reanimating her. The 'hulking half-ton' slab didn't protect her from grave robbers though and poor Lillias's remains were divvied out among universities and antiquarian collectors.

From the beach, we scrambled over the low wall to the roadside beside the railway bridge and found the plaque remembering Lillias, lying on the verge in line with her grave slab. Finding the beautiful bronze disc in the grass was like stumbling upon treasure. It's illustrated with Adie's face and a surround of plants, Torryburn buildings, a crescent moon and a prancing devil. 'They feared she would rise from the dead', it reads. 'How could she as she was an ordinary woman.' We spent a few moments contemplating Lillias's life and unjust fate, the disc a portal to a past that felt strangely less distant.

Its location is not at all obvious, and less determined adventurers may not have found it. The Valleyfield plaque proved even more elusive. We stopped dozens of people as we trudged along the coastal path in the rain, the May afternoon having turned suddenly dark. They were unfailingly friendly and wanted to be helpful. Some knew of the Torryburn and Culross ones but none that their local plaque sits under the information boards at the entrance to Valleyfield Woods, as we discovered driving back up the road later. This one also remembers Adie, 'an innocent victim of unenlightened times'. As we lingered, a bus pulled up and deposited a walking group, who congregated near the boards. We willed them to look down and notice the plaque. Nobody did.

There's no missing the Culross one. It's under the information board by the bus stop facing the Town Hall. One of writer Sara Sheridan's 'Witches Unite' stickers marks the spot. The heritage village of Culross's cobbled streets, tiny houses and terracotta-coloured palace with a wee café tucked in behind it mask its bloody history. With a population of about six hundred people in the 1600s, this small community murdered thirty-two of its women. 'So many ordinary women', reads the plaque.

The lives of the women, the brutal times they lived in and their restless ghosts were brought vividly to life for us by Linda from the National Trust for Scotland. She pointed out the tiny top-floor windows of the Town House, where the accused were imprisoned and tortured. They apparently still make their presence felt with otherworldly noises and unexplained incidents. They're not at peace and we don't blame them for still raging at the injustices and indignities they suffered.

On International Women's Day 2022, then-First Minister Nicola Sturgeon issued a state apology for the witch trials, followed later by an apology from the Church of Scotland. Work is ongoing to issue a legal pardon of the victims of this massive-scale miscarriage of justice. Maybe then they'll rest. Maybe.

Author note: *The story is about a mapless walk along the Fife Witches Trail and the adventures we had along the way.*

The Den in the Forest
Jo Higgs

My grandma had a cottage at the foot of Glen Lyon in Perthshire. It was a cosy little place, nestled onto the far end of a row of cottages, leaning into sparse fields and crowded from behind by a sprawling forest. This forest was a utopia to a nine-year-old like myself, and a seven-year-old like my sister. Every day we snuck beyond the lichen-spotted gate of the back garden to go explore the real garden.

We would hardly be a few metres into the trees before moss, dirt, ferns, ticks, broken branches and sharp gusts of wind would rouse our senses and spin us into a glorious world of endless adventure. For many, the idea of adventure has to be premised on a sense of newness – for us, we could repeat the same actions, follow the same paths we had stomped into the earth ourselves, notice the same quirks of nature and never lose the vitality of the adventure. Repetitiveness had no dampening effect on the excitement the environment gave us.

As we jaunted up the gentle slope we would use the same markers over and over again to ensure we found the correct route: 'There's that big stone with the crack I got my foot stuck in, turn left!'; 'Okay, just through that huge rhododendron bush'; 'D'ye want to go up or around the scrambling rock-face?'; 'Oh – that's the tree stump where we thought that bee was going to sting us. Too far. Back that way!'

We recycled our nature, never draining it of fun by five, ten or a hundred of the same observations. We'd scoop up big branches draped with withering skeleton leaves and, with the length of them sitting on one of our shoulders each, walk them up to the den. Sometimes when we reached the den the cuffs of our jeans would be full of mud, and we'd squelch as we crouched down to fit into it.

The den was an upturned tree, wrenched out of its earth by a storm years ago. Its roots reached out in front itself, slowly drooping back down to tickle the dirt they used to sit in – nature, in its beautiful way of doing things, left an entrance just about our size, so we made it more homely by padding out the roof with leaves to bring shelter and shoving branches in to strengthen the structure. I would enter first to crouch in the den, sitting as light sparkled in through gaps and thin leaves, and my sister would linger in the entrance complaining there wasn't quite enough room for both of us. I would give her a turn going in on her own and she would smile and footer about with the slaters and slugs we shared the den with.

On brisk days the leaves would whistle and hush, only to be drowned out by calls of 'lunch is ready, come on!' from a few hundred metres away. So we'd leave our den for another day and run back along the familiar route, still getting fun and excitement out of the journey but perhaps slightly distracted by the warm thought of chicken broth.

Author note: *My grandma's cottage gave me some pretty foundational memories and experiences. The forest up the back was beautiful and provided a playground for me and my sister that we were so lucky to have when we could visit. We made our way up to the den nearly every day we were there to just play and hang about (most of the time our parents did follow us up – but occasionally we snuck up on our own).*

The Camping Pee
Hazel Knox

Fumbling around in the dark, I wonder when I morphed into a caterpillar, but this isn't an insect body – it's a sleeping bag and I have a bigger problem. Every camper's nightmare is my miserable reality. It's the middle of the night and I need to pee.

Flipping over, I face my happily snoring brother. If only we could swap places: me blissfully asleep, his bladder begging to be emptied. Maybe if I lie on my back…

No, that's worse.

If I curl up?

Nope.

If I curl up and think about deserts?

Still need a pee.

I don't. I just need to get back to sleep. Closing my eyes, I visualise myself in peaceful slumber… on an inflatable raft, floating down a river, a waterfall gushing nearby. Argh! I need a pee and I need it bad. I hate camping.

I wriggle out of the sleeping bag, bouncing my snoozing brother on the shared lilo. Scrabbling around for a torch and jumper, I trip over the folded chairs dragged in from last night's rain. My feet are in my wellies before I remember they too were brought in mid-shower. A zip fumble, doorway stumble and I'm squelching my way to the toilet block.

Aaaaaaaaaaaaahhh!

Every inch of my body celebrates the relief. When I

70

stroll back the pinky edges of dawn are peeking through. Two fox cubs play-fight metres from our tent, knocking droplets of dew off the long grass. The tent zip slides open and I kick my wellies off. The jumper stays on and soon I'm warm and cosy, back in caterpillar pose. My brother has turned over so the only noises are the tent flapping and birds beginning to sing. I shut my eyes, content knowing I won't have to pee again for hours. Unlike my brother, who will wake needing one.

I love camping.

Author note: *As a child, we went on annual camping holidays to the west coast of Scotland. My bladder was small and middle-of-the-night stumbles to the toilet block were a regular occurrence.*

Welly Diving
Nicole Carter

We trekked over hill and dale
for several hours
in the baking August sun
our destination turned out to be
a pretty hefty high-level gorge
none o' yer kiddies' stuff here
this was go hard or go home
character-building, apparently
and I was having
the time of my life
a good distraction from having
to stay at the homeless hostel
after running away from home
again

Bedecked in wellies
and not-so-waterproofs
our gorge walk was precarious
and actually dangerous
if you weren't concentrating intently
on where you placed your feet
and wet fingers on the
often slippy, algae-covered sandstone

Eventually, our instructor
stopped us at a point where
there was a waterfall with
a very deep peaty pool beneath
and announced that we were to

jump in
considering
the other activities we'd done
over the past two weeks
I wasn't surprised

Each of us took our turn to jump in
many losing one or both wellies
in the process
a couple of the guys tried to
dive down to retrieve them
but to no avail
each time they resurfaced
with the wrong size

I wasn't hopeful of my chances of
keeping mine, when it was my turn
sure enough
I lost one on the first jump
losing the second one whilst
trying to retrieve it
It was a welly graveyard down there
the remains from many others'
previous expeditions
The Depths, Baltic with a capital 'B'
despite the summer heat

After several attempts at
diving down, only to resurface
with the wrong size each time
eventually resolving myself to
the fact I couldn't retrieve a size 7
so had to squelch all the way
back to the centre

with two different-sized wellies on
heartened only by the fact
that everyone else
including the instructor
was doing the same

Author note: *A snippet of one of the adventures I had
when I did the Outward Bound classic course in the
Lake District in 2000, thanks to Venture Scotland and
Cyrenians. I'm settled now, thanks to my family and The
City of Edinburgh Council.*

Wild Swimming in the Mareel
Charlotte Anderson

If you google 'mareel' the first thing that will come up in your search is the state-of-the-art entertainment venue in Lerwick, Shetland. An excellent venue for sure, but that is not what mareel actually is.

Mareel is phosphorescence in the sea that appears during late summer into autumn (marr = sea, and eldr = fire in Old Norn). In the past it has been attributed to dragons and gods across Asia and a sign of premonition for the Romans. Phosphorescence is created by tiny marine organisms which glow in the dark when oxygen is dissolved in the water around them.

More often associated with warm tropical islands, it is actually found all across the UK as well. If you speak to anyone who makes their living around the sea, they will probably have seen it at some point in their life, but many have never heard of it.

Cut to 1 September 2021 around 10pm, a calm night, when car headlights can be seen moving slowly down a single-track road and parking out of the way. Engines are switched off and it is dark once more in Ollaberry. Out climb folk in dark waterproof cloaks, or even their dressing gowns, with head torches on. People say hello to each other but, in the darkness, it is hard to see who is who. Head torches just blind folk. Differentiating folk by their voices is the only way. Someone asks if this is some kind of cult as more gather at the top of a garden. Light suddenly floods out of an open door as two folk come out into the night; not sure if they were in the right place they had popped inside for a yarn.

An excited chatter fills the air. The cloud cover makes the sky very dark, no stars or moon out to guide the way. New and experienced sea swimmers alike have been brought together tonight in search of something a bit mysterious. The group begin to move down through the green gate at the bottom of the garden and jump down onto the sand, feet sinking in. It is an extremely low tide. The ridges of wave ripples have been imprinted into the beach as the tide ebbed and sea glass glints when it catches the light from a torch. Once everyone has reached the edge of the water, bags and shoes are set down, everyone disrobes, standing in their swimwear looking to the dark sea, and the head torches are switched off.

The group begin to make their way into the chilly North Sea. Everyone is quiet, looking down at their feet as they slowly wade out into the water. A sudden shriek from the left: 'My feet are glowing!' Everyone starts to kick their feet and exclaim in disbelief as their feet turn a pale green. The bravest of the group start swimming out while the more unsure stand up to their thighs in the water trying to acclimatise to the cold water and give a squeal when something unknown brushes against their leg.

'I'm going in! Who's coming with me? After 3. 1… 2… 3!'

When you take the plunge, the sudden cold pushes all the air out of your lungs. Some shriek, some make no audible sound, breathing quickly, trying to get more air into their lungs, and some appear as if they have just dived into a heated pool, the cool water having no effect. After a while your body adjusts, and the water feels therapeutic, bringing your heart rate down.

As you swim a bit deeper, the mareel becomes brighter. With each movement of your arms, it is as though the water is full of shimmering glitter or fireflies or stars, something a bit magical and equally hard to explain. Treading water, you can see your arms and legs glowing pale green under the surface, surrounded by these tiny organisms. The cold water is both relaxing and invigorating, creating a sense of balance within you. The low chatter of the group, still in complete amazement at what they are seeing, is only broken by an occasional squeal when someone has swum through a patch of seaweed, drooie-lines wrapping around their limbs, proving difficult to shake off. Is this what a grindylow gripping your leg would be like?

Time seems to come to a standstill as you float around in the dark sea, watching the mareel swirl around you. Not a breath of wind to even ruffle the water. Although you are in with a group of people, everyone is self-contained in their own little bubble, watching the water beneath themselves. But of course, time is not standing still, and your feet and hands begin to go numb. It is time to leave the enchanting world of the mareel that made you feel like an ethereal mermaid and return to the land. Ungracefully wading through the shallows, breaking the muffled darkness as you splash up the beach, you have a sudden appreciation for the selkies that wiggle their way ashore.

Everyone tries to rub some warmth back into their skin with their towels, pulling on their robes, which stick to their damp skin. The group slowly amble back up the beach again, turning their backs to the sea, leaving the mareel in peace until another night.

Share your love of books. . .

Scottish Book Trust is an independent national charity. Our mission is to ensure people living in Scotland have equal access to books.

If you're enjoying this book, please consider making a donation so that everyone in Scotland has the opportunity to improve their life chances through books and the fundamental skills of reading and writing.

Visit **scottishbooktrust.com/donate** to find out more.

A Floral Tribute
Sarah Rushbrooke

You're not meant to make life-altering decisions when a loved one dies. But I did.

Back in 2017, my grandma came to visit me in Glasgow. I knew then that it would be her final adventure. As we climbed the wonky steps of the tenement, she gripped my hand tightly, her rings digging into my flesh. A draught came from that one wooden sash window that no one could close. I swung open the front door, revealing my new home to her.

She dabbed her eyes with her handkerchief, a blue CB stitched in one corner. 'It's beautiful, Sarah.'

My partner and I took her on a bright red bus that served afternoon tea. Happy birthday banners decorated the table we were seated at.

'But whose birthday is it?' Grandma kept whispering to me.

'It was yours, a few weeks ago.' I'd whisper back. She'd nod, take a sip of prosecco, watch out the window as Glasgow whizzed by, then she'd turn to me again: 'But whose birthday is it?'

Afterwards we drove up to Loch Lomond. Julie Andrews joined us in the car for a singalong: 'Raindrops on roses and whiskers on kittens!' We found a bench close to the water's edge. She pulled me near and wrapped her cream knit shawl around our shoulders. I nestled into her; I smelt talc and lilacs. The evening sun pierced through the clouds, streaks of gold were painted across the loch. A small boat bobbed gently in the water.

Months of lockdowns and restrictions had me dreading Christmas. It would be the first festive season I'd spent away from my family. I WhatsApped friends asking if they'd all chip in for some foliage and I'd show them how to make a seasonal wreath on Zoom. It had been nearly a decade since I'd worked in a florist and created with my hands.

I filled the bath with cold water. Secateurs back in hand, I was transported back to that fifteen-year-old who conditioned boxes of roses, chrysanthemums and carnations every Saturday morning. I slipped off the elastic bands from each bundle of foliage and snipped the stems. I plunged the greenery deep in the water to rehydrate. I watched as woody conifer branches turned my fingers black and the eucalyptus left behind sticky sap. The bathroom filled with relaxing spa-like scents of fresh pine. I took deep, deep breaths, filling my lungs. It smelt like nostalgia and new beginnings.

I laid out the damp foliage across my kitchen floor, portioning it out so each person received their share. Occasionally my deer-like dog would hop between the bundles, her nose deep amongst the leaves, intrigued by all the new smells. I stabbed a sharp blade into the thick plastic bag of moss, the knife easily sliced it open and revealed green, earthy guts. Bugs and beasties made their escape as I started to pull apart clumps of the moss.

A seed of excitement started to take root as I dropped off bags of foliage and moss to my friends. A day later, when they all joined the Zoom call, I came alive.

'You could do this. Like as a job,' a friend said, as I was showing everyone how to tie a buoyant bow for their wreaths. I was years deep into a marketing career. I wasn't unhappy, but I wasn't happy either.

*

Three months later I got the call. I'd been running a bath, I'd poured in too many bubbles and had stripped to my underwear.

'This looks like the end, Sarah,' my mum told me. I don't know how I replied.

Clinging to the side of the toilet bowl, my knees stinging from the uncomfortable tiles, vomit and tears poured out of me. Minutes and then hours and then days stretched by, waiting by my phone. Covid restrictions still loomed and I wasn't allowed to travel back home.

I kept thinking of all those times she'd said: 'Don't come and visit me. Get on with your life. I don't want you to see me when I'm old and wrinkly.' She was so earnest.

I'd burst out laughing. 'You're already old and wrinkly, Grandma,' She tutted, then dissolved into laughter.

Against my will I was obeying her wishes.

Long ago I'd offered to make her a heart-shaped floral tribute, overflowing with pale pink, frothy carnations. Her favourite flower. I joined a friend from floristry college in her Derbyshire studio. She worked on Grandma's casket spray, brimming with purple alliums and fuchsia snapdragons. Beside her I fluffed out the carnations. I kept blinking away tears, but my fingertips fizzled with delight. This was where I belonged, amongst flowers. Mere weeks after her funeral I was hunting for a part-time job. The seed of excitement the wreath workshop had planted in me was sprouting rapidly. Part-time employment would give me the chance to grow a small business. If Grandma were still here, I knew she would be encouraging me.

At the end of 2021, I stood in front of a class of fourteen, most of them strangers.

'Thanks so much for coming along,' I said. 'I can't wait to see how each of your wreaths turns out.' A bead of sweat ran down the side of my face and my mouth felt dry. But the smile wouldn't leave my face. I'd spent sleepless nights refreshing the Eventbrite page on my phone, panicking tickets wouldn't sell. But they had.

This year's wedding season began in an explosion of pinks, blues and yellows. Buckets were filled to the brim with cheerful camomiles and wiggly-stemmed poppies. As I constructed a bridal bouquet, I noticed a Polaroid pinned to my wall. Me and my grandma; I'm holding a bottle of cheap champagne and she's raising a full glass. It felt like she was toasting my new beginnings. A few weeks later I typed out the resignation letter for my part-time job. Here begins the next step in my floral adventure.

Author note: *Me and my grandma were best friends. She died during 2021 and it gave me the shake I needed to return to a passion of mine: floristry. I began a part-time business and over the last two years it's blossomed. Even though she's gone, my grandma is still instrumental in my life.*

Route 90
Stranraer Open Book Creative Writing Group
By Gillian, Jane, Jean, Joan, Nikki and Kathryn

As I set out –
I hope I can read my maps.
I hope I have packed enough snacks.

As I set out –
I see pebbles, small and glittery.
I see pebbles grow larger, sharper and more difficult.

As I set out –
I know my best friend will meet me at the end.
I know I will enjoy my time with her.

As I set out –
I learn that small things don't matter.
I learn that I can live life differently.

As I set out –
I feel free. It's an escape.
I feel no sadness.

As I set out –
I welcome unspeakable beauty and deep wisdom.
I welcome Fear as it passes by me and I journey on.

Don't turn back.
The house is empty.

An Ode to Wanderlust
Sumayya Usmani

This has always been my favourite café in London, especially during springtime. I spent so many warmer days here when I lived in London, a time when I felt melancholic about how I was passing my life by in my thirties as a lawyer. I'd look out from the full-length windows, taking in the ephemeral beauty of floral baskets dangling from the Victorian lampposts thinking of how I longed to make a career out of something creative instead.

As I take a sip of my nearly cold cappuccino, I'm distracted by the effervescence of teenage university students sitting at the table on my left talking about job fairs and internships. I pretend not to listen while pushing away the twinge of regret that lost time often conjures up – what if I had chosen differently three decades ago? I turned fifty a couple of months ago and all I seem to be doing is indulging in monumental self-reflection. What if I had studied creative writing instead of law, and begun a career in writing when I was twenty instead of forty? Wouldn't I have been more financially secure and fulfilled now? The questions block my writing flow so I resort to you, my diary, instead.

Maybe our true calling doesn't always fall into our laps at eighteen, maybe you need to live a little before it finds you. A lot of how I've figured out life's decisions has been by trusting my intuition and by returning to writing. Writing was always a place of solace, somewhere that my thoughts could come alive without judgement.

From those lonely years on and off merchant vessels as a child to when I settled in Pakistan – a country that was meant to feel like home but never did – it seems that the only place I felt at home was before an empty diary page. You never offered unhelpful advice or told me what path to take, what you did was allow me to let go of trying to be someone I wasn't – even though I didn't realise that then.

At fifty I have many questions, fears and hopes, dear diary. Is it too late for me now? Am I on a career path that has now passed me by and I won't have fulfilled my golden years?

By fifty wasn't I supposed to have figured life out?

Childhood never felt permanent, followed by an adolescence of wrong relationships and even worse friendships. In Pakistan I was battling against conformity. I tried and failed marriage as a means of escape from the expectations of being a Pakistani woman. Why couldn't I just be like everyone else?

What if I had reached towards writing earlier? But law was the expected, sensible choice and so I dulled my creative spark. There were moments when I'd see myself shine as I took on new hobbies and artistic endeavours – but expectation arrested my progress each time. I was torn between other people's definitions of an ideal life and not knowing who I really was.

'Find a career that fits you, makes you who you are,' that's what Daddy always said. I used to envy my peers as I watched them growing up and finding their calling. I never felt that way about the law. Each day at university I felt my intellect was lacking because I couldn't grasp most concepts. I got away with convincing people I understood law with my big mouth and my ostensibly ambitious nature. I spent so long pretending that I almost convinced myself creativity really wasn't my calling and was probably best left as a hobby.

But here I am, dear diary, on the precipice of change. Will the longing for words and wanderlust lead me to true freedom? Am I out of my depth? What if I fail?

But there are times I know this path feels right: when creativity enters my body as electricity I have never felt before, when shivers run down my back as words flow because they want to and not because I need them to. I know that words are my freedom when I read what I've written and am in awe of my own potential to tell stories.

Is respecting my own talent the door to adventure I so seek?

So here I am with writing guiding me into a brave new world. But it doesn't mean I'm not battling disbelief and fear. Is it too late, does becoming a writer at fifty mean anything, or is it just the first drop in the ocean of the future I'm meant to have? So now, as I step into the skin I was born for, I find myself naturally following that trusted friend: my intuition. This year I take a leap towards the future I have longed for: a master's degree in creative writing and working on ideas for future books that I've often scribbled in my journals.

Maybe this is the secret to eternal adventure: self-belief and not letting age be crippling. People say I don't look my age. Maybe it's because I'm still filled with the exuberance of adolescence. I look over to the excited teenagers at the table across from me and smile. I see the feigned confidence I too once had and then I look at my reflection in the window and I recognise this woman now. I'm the woman I want to be.

As I pay the bill and gather my belongings to step into the early spring sunshine, I accept that finding yourself

Zugzwang
John Lockhart

In chess, it's called 'zugzwang'… when the only viable
   move… is not to move,
In life it's called by many names, sometimes worse as
   one gets older.
The comfortable flat, familiar decor, pictures on the wall,
   I have nothing to prove,
Except there is a thought that lives behind tired Netflix
   eyes, a call to be bolder.

Airport drop-off parking is timed, limited conversation
   for goodbye, I hold her tight,
My daughter takes a photograph, text added 'and he's
   off' posted to the family group chat.
Years before roles reversed, off to teach English, my joy,
   my fears followed her Asia flight,
Earth will travel halfway around the sun before I return,
   many an unfamiliar habitat.

A small, loved country recedes in the aeroplane window,
   higher now, I gaze at sculptured cloud formations,
My mind wanders, time to be alone, time to reflect on
   the days that went before.
The baggage I have carried for so long, now time to
   jettison this limiting cargo,
Look with new eyes, hear new sounds, test out my own
   flawed expectations.

Author note: *I have just completed the first month of six months of travel around Asia. I'm writing this in New Delhi just before heading to the airport for Nepal. At sixty-one, I have thought about taking time to travel, and I have thought of many reasons not to. So it is an adventure not just in visiting new countries, but also leaving my now grown-up family behind for the first time.*

Veracity
Rosemary Henderson

It was cold. So cold.

I was bundled up in a dirty, black duffle coat, two sizes too big for me, with only two toggles still attached. The scent of my mother's cigarettes clung to everything I wore, woven into the fibres of my clothes, smelling both sharp and stale. I hated that smell, the way it invaded my senses, burning my eyes and making everything feel grimy. Other kids, the ones whose parents didn't light up as soon as their eyes opened, would wrinkle their nose at me, step back as I approached as though my scent could be caught.

'She smells,' it would begin.

'She's dirty.'

'Look at her hair.'

'Look at her nails.'

'Do you even know what a bath is?' they would ask, surrounding me, taunting me, as though I'd made the choice to look this way. Dress this way. Exist like this.

Quietly closing the large, black gate behind me so I didn't disturb anyone, I began my short journey to school, heading towards the beach.

There was snow on the ground; I hadn't seen it here before. I had seen snow of course – two houses ago? No, three houses ago, when I had a different name and lived in Wales. The snow would fall thick and fast there, and when you opened the front door you were met with a wall of white, just the imprint of the front door left behind. My uncle would dig to get into us, calling out

93

my name and making the laborious effort of digging through the snow into a game. I would use my bucket and spade from our summer beach trips, shovelling snow into my little yellow bucket and running it through to the bathroom, dumping it in the bath and running straight back, seeing who could break through first. It was usually him, with my gran at his shoulder, pulling me into a tight embrace then tossing me in the air as if I were weightless. I felt loved. Reassured. I was safe.

*

I could feel the cold through my shoes, my socks already uncomfortably damp from the holes in my soles. I needed to get to school, the radiators would be on this morning and my teacher had put me right beside the one at the window, the best seat in the classroom, she said. I could tuck my shoes underneath to dry, and rest my feet on the radiator, dissolving the chill that currently runs through my body.

Walking faster, I reached the bottom of the street. I wrapped my arms tight around me, drawing my coat tightly closed, braced for the wind to literally take my breath away like it did most mornings.

I'm not sure what made me look up. Usually, I walked with my head down. No one noticed me that way. It made me feel invisible, avoiding the pitying looks from other mums, their whispers following me as I made the solo walk to school. I'm glad I did.

It was... beautiful! The sand was covered in a pristine layer of snow, shimmering as though someone had spilled a pot of glitter over the entire beach and promenade.

The horizon was a symphony of colours – gentle blue,

soft pink and warm orange. Transcending the freezing temperature, defying the winter chill. Below it, the gentle ebb and flow of the sea resembled a rhythmic dance. Gracefully, the waves teased the shoreline before retreating, gradually covering more of the snow-covered sand.

I made my way to the promenade wall, sitting down, not caring about the chill that was about to spread up my spine. I wanted to capture it all, keep this feeling of joy, of being at one with the world.

Inhaling, the crisp winter air filled my lungs with a freshness they hadn't felt for a long time.

Exhaling, I imagined that the mist-like tendrils of vapour meeting the cold air were the extraction of the thick tobacco smoke that never left my lungs.

Inhale. Exhale. Deep breath in. Cleansing breath out.

Feeling lighter, I got to my feet and began the balancing act of walking along the wall, one foot in front of the other, stopping every few steps to look at the footprints I had left behind.

I was forbidden from doing this. It was part of a long, long list of rules I had to follow, many of which made no sense to me. I was her biggest mistake, she would spit at me when I messed up or let a secret slip out. Her voice felt like nails on a chalkboard, using words that hurt my soul more than her hands could hurt my body, always removing one of her slippers towards the end of her tirade. When she calmed down, she would write a note excusing me from PE until my bruises faded.

But this taste of rebellion was exhilarating. Of all the rules, this felt like the least dangerous to break. The most dangerous, of course, was...

No.

But maybe, yes.

No one was around. The only footprints in the snow were mine.

Dropping off the wall, I pulled my hand out of the warmth and safety of my sleeve. My hand trembled, adrenaline coursing through my veins.

Slowly, fearful of being caught, I used my index finger to write in the snow. It took seconds.

Stepping back, I looked at what I'd written.

Rosemary Reilly.

I couldn't feel my finger, it was so cold. I examined it, wiggling back and forward. I looked at my name, the real one, engraved in the snow. My finger did that.

Turning towards school, I heard the bell ring. I took a quick look back before running past the amusements, past the tower that looked like a castle's turret and into the playground. Leaving my secret written in the snow.

Author note: *During a winter morning walk to school along Portobello Promenade, a fresh layer of snow felt as though nature had hit the reset button on my surroundings. This inspired an act of rebellion, giving me back my identity for a short time that I still cherish many years later.*

Ainm Ùr
Victoria Maciver

Cliog, cliog is tha thu a-staigh
sàbhailte, sèimh is socair.
Coisichidh sinn a-mach an doras
an dòchas
nach tillidh sinn idir.

Thug thu dhomh ainm ùr
nuair a' ràinig thu
ro thràth
dà mhìos roimhe.

Nuair a choinnich sinn
eadar uinneag chruaidh
ann an taigh-ghlainne
gun lusan
no aiteas.

Chuala mi an rèidio ciùin
a' cluich
le fuaim na h-innealan.
Am fàileadh geur
a dh' ionnsaigh orm
mar meanbh-chuileagan
as t-Fhoghar.

Do dhealbh nam phòcaid
cho faiceallach
preusant on dotair ciallach.

'On oidhche a dh' fhalbh thu
sa bhogsa plastaig
an dithis againn ar fàgail
aonranach.

Ach dh' fhàs thu làidir
is dh' fhàs thu slàn
san àite a thachair
sinn còmhla.

Choisich mi a-steach nam 'Tori'
ach dh' fhàg mi nam Mhamaidh.
An t-ainm ùr as fheàrr leam
as motha.
An diugh, sa màireach
gu siorraidh.

A new name

Click, click and you are in
safe, calm and gentle.
We will walk out the door
hoping
never to return.

You gave me a new name
when you arrived
too early
two months before.

When we met
between a hard window
in a greenhouse
without growth
or joy.

I heard the radio quietly
humming
with the sound of the machines.
The pungent smell
wafting towards me
like midges
in autumn.

Your picture in my pocket
so carefully
a present from the wise doctor.
Since the night you left
in the plastic box
the two of us left
lonely.

But you grew strong
and you grew whole
in the place
where we met together.
I walked in as 'Tori'
but I left as Mammy.
The new name I prefer
most.
Today, and tomorrow
forever.

Author note: *Walking out of Raigmore Hospital after having my first son, born two months premature. Following a stay in the Special Care Baby Unit (SCBU) given his very early arrival, it was like leaving a goldfish bowl and taking a breath of fresh air. I was a new person, with a new name.*

Continue the adventure

Want to read more?

The full collection of almost 250 Adventure stories is available to read on our website, together with more Scotland's Stories from previous years.

Scan the QR code or visit
scottishbooktrust.com/scotlands-stories

Share your love of books. . .

Scottish Book Trust is an independent national charity. Our mission is to ensure people living in Scotland have equal access to books.

If you've enjoyed this book, please consider making a donation so that everyone in Scotland has the opportunity to improve their life chances through books and the fundamental skills of reading and writing.

Visit **scottishbooktrust.com/donate** to find out more.

Previous editions

We have published an annual collection of stories like this one every year since 2009.

Days Like This (2009)
The Book That Changed My Life (2010)
Scottish Family Legends (2011)
My Favourite Place (2012)
Treasures (2013)
Scotland's Stories of Home (2014)
Journeys (2015)
Secrets and Confessions (2016)
Nourish (2017)
Rebel (2018)
Blether (2019)
Future (2020)
Celebration (2021)
Scotland's Stories (2022)